Discipleship Books:

80 Spiritual Principles

By

Philip Watson

Dedication

Dedicated to my loving wife Dianne, and my three children, Andrew, Jonathon and Ruth.

My grateful thanks for allowing me to spend so much of my spare time writing these words.

Acknowledgments

My grateful thanks to Warren Portsmouth who patiently helped me review the manuscripts of my books. Warren suggested improvements and asked questions at appropriate points.

I also want to acknowledge the help of the Holy Spirit for inspiring me to write these books and for frequently reminding me of scriptures, relevant to topics, in each book.

Books about Jesus:

He Changed Our World
The Ministry of Jesus
The Incarnation
The Son
Attitude In Jesus' Teachings (soon to be published)

Other books written by Philip Watson:

Humility
Great Summaries
The Holy Spirit

Books Coming Soon

1200 Great Quotes
Attitude In the Old Testament
Attitude In Acts, Epistles and Revelation
Evidence The Bible Is True
Creation or Evolution
The Father

Table of Contents

Introduction

We are spiritual beings and the Bible is a spiritual book! Whenever I read an analysis of the content of the Bible, I usually find the content described, like this. The Bible contains a variety of books written by different authors and over thousands of years. The content includes: history, prophecy, psalms, poetry, proverbs, teachings, parables and law. What is inevitably missing from those summaries, are words like these. The Bible is a record of different individuals

spiritual experiences and *spiritual insights* and *spiritual principles.*

A record of experiences, insights and principles; that helped God's people in the Old Testament and Christians in the New Testament, to understand the nature of the Father/Son/ and Holy Spirit and have a relationship with them.

What do I mean by *spiritual experiences*? There are too many to list, but following on are some examples. Think of Jonah hearing God's voice, not liking the task he had been asked to do and subsequently; taking a boat and to try and run away from God's call - as if God could not see him taking the boat, or know where he was going! Or Jonah, wishing that he could die because God had been merciful to the city of Ninevah after he had preached repentance there, and God causing a flower to grow and then die.

Jonah's experience and lessons were threefold. Firstly, God loves even wicked cities and wicked people. Secondly, God would rather be merciful to them. Thirdly, you cannot run away from God.

Then, think of Elijah, telling his servant to go look for clouds on the horizon and it was only on the seventh time that his servant saw the clouds, and then Elijah new the rain he had predicted, was coming. However it required the servant to go 6 times before the evidence finally began to appear on the horizon. A principle that reiterates what Jesus said, "ask and keep on asking" and a parable Jesus told about a man who persistently asked his neighbour for help – as a means of saying. God does listen to our prayers, but the answer may not be the first time we ask. It might be the seventh time.

Or the story of Elisha and a widow who's late husband's creditors were seeking to take away her two sons as payment. The moving story of how she came to Elijah, the man of God for help. Then the story took a twist, most of us would not expect. Elijah told the widow in debt to ask her neighbours for any empty storage jars, then start pouring oil from the one jar of oil she had, into the jars borrowed from neighbours till these borrowed jars were full. Then she went and sold the oil, to pay off her debts.

This widow, out of her faith in God and his servant Elijah asked for help then followed the instructions she had received, and saw a miracle of provision. God could have dropped the money to repay her debts from heaven, instead chose to ask her to participate in the miracle. This miracle, was a fore-runner to the multiplication of the loaves and fishes that occurred during the ministry of Jesus. Jesus could have prayed, God please drop the bread from heaven. Instead, Jesus asked the disciples what they had. They told him, "5 loaves and 2 fish". Both miracles started with what they had, and God multiplied what they had.

Or think of Samuel's mother before Samuel was conceived, praying with such distress that the Priest thought she was drunk – and God graciously answering her prayer. And think of Samuel, while still a boy, hearing a voice in the night and thinking that it must be the old priest Eli, calling. Then finally, after the third time, the Old Priest realised that it was God who was talking to the boy.

Or Anna, prompted by the Holy Spirit to go to the Temple to see the baby Jesus – the Son of God. Or Peter who had a vision in which he saw 'unclean' animals being lowered three times. That vision was given because Jesus wanted Peter to consider Gentiles as people God loved also.

The Bible is 'full' of people's, spiritual experiences. Some heard God speak during the night, such as Samuel. Saul heard Jesus speak to him during the day, while on the road. Philip heard the Holy Spirit speak while walking beside a chariot carrying an important official in it. Some met with angels while others had visions of angels. Others had dreams or were transported in the Spirit. Others, simply waited on God, in prayer.

The focus of this book will be *spiritual insights* and *spiritual principles (or laws)* that emerge from these experiences and spiritual principles that were revealed to various people in the Bible. If we recognise these *spiritual insights* and *spiritual principles* and apply them to our lives – we will benefit from the experiences of those who have, gone before us.

What do I mean by a *spiritual insight* or a *spiritual principle*? Let me give one example. James wrote.

> "Draw near to God, and God will draw near to you."

That is a *spiritual insight* and also a *spiritual principle.* That principle tells us how God acts towards people. That (spiritual) principle tells us that if someone has not previously had a relationship with God, when they sincerely turn towards God, because he knows what is on their hearts, he comes running towards them.

That principle *"Draw near to God, and God will draw near to you",* applies equally to anyone who is a committed Christian. Sometimes, we Christians, allow the demands of life to crowd God out. Yet, graciously, as soon as we start turning their thoughts towards him, he comes running in much the same way the father of the prodigal son came running towards his wayward son.

That same spiritual principle, tells us a lot about the nature of God. That is, he will never 'force' anyone to believe in him or have a relationship with him. God, in his grace, will wait patiently for us to turn our hearts and thoughts towards him. But as soon we turn our hearts and thoughts towards him (because he knows what is in our heart and our thinking; and that the door is open), graciously he comes towards us, to meet with us.

Throughout the Bible, there are *spiritual laws* and *spiritual principles* like that one. It would be helpful if they were all listed in one place but because the Bible is book written by 60 different authors and over thousands of years, those spiritual laws and principles are scattered between Genesis and Revelation.

There are six truths this book is based on.
1. Jesus said, "the words I speak, they are spirit and they are life." John 6:63 A paraphrase of those words of Jesus, is this. If you are spiritually perceptive, my words are spiritual food, and by eating them (that is listening to them, then believing and applying them), you will find life!
2. We are: *spiritual beings* and we have been given a *spirit* by God. See John 3:6 and Romans 8:16. Pierre Tilhard de Chardin wrote.
    > *We are not human beings having a spiritual experience but 'spiritual' beings having a human experience.*

3. We Christians have been given the Holy Spirit to help us understand spiritual truths. Both Jesus and the

Apostle Paul agreed on that point. Jesus said, "the *Spirit* (Holy Spirit) gives birth to *spirit* (our human spirit)." John 3:6 The Apostle Paul was on the same wave length when he wrote "The *Spirit* (Holy Spirit) testifies with our *spirit*.... Rom 8:16

4. We only gain spiritual insight and recognise *spiritual truths* and *spiritual principles,* because the Holy Spirit has 'revealed' them to us. Paul writing about God's secret wisdom, wrote. "But God has revealed it to us by his Spirit." 1 Cor 2:10 The Apostle did not write about God's wisdom after repeatedly reading the Old Testament from cover to cover and then finally, drawing a conclusion. Or understand God's wisdom as a result of a deep discussion with one of the great teachers of the time. He recognised the wisdom of God because the Holy Spirit had 'revealed' it to him.

When the Holy Spirit 'reveals' truth to us, that revelation, often does not occur with a blinding flash. Often it is when we are alone and listening or praying or reading the Bible. Then when we are receptive, the Holy Spirit will reveal a truth to us. Or it may be while singing a hymn or chorus that the Holy Spirit witnesses with our spirit, as if to say.

Those words were not penned because the person writing them, was a brilliant author or had exceptional insight. The person who wrote those words, wrote under the inspiration of the Holy Spirit.

When the Spirit reveals truth to us, he is prompting us to recognise that we have been reading, *Spirit inspired* truth.

5. Opposed to anything God does and anything Christians do, is a being called satan. He has an army of unseen servants, called demons. It is fashionable today, to dismiss demons as beings, only primitive peoples believed in but that now in our so-called, 'enlightened times', the existence of Satan and demons can be dismissed as possibly belonging to the paranormal or beings that are conjured up in the minds of people who have some form of psychosis.

This is not the place to give a full explanation of demons or their role, but we Christians who are committed to do the will of God, have to realise that there is an opposing force and need to be aware of that possibility. But also, we have the weapons and words and power to defeat, that opposing force, quite easily. See the section on Warfare.

6. We humans were made for relationships. With God. With each

other. With ourselves (to be true to our self and honest with our self) and with our environment.

This book is a collection of spiritual truths and principles the Holy Spirit has revealed to me, over many years. Now I have to admit, I do not regard myself as a particularly 'spiritual' Christian. I am more like the carnal Christian Paul wrote about. Someone who prefers to spend their spare time watching sports or reading books, rather than praying or reading the Bible.

If I have recognised spiritual truth and spiritual principles, it is primarily because of the graciousness of God who asked his Holy Spirit to reveal them to me, in spite of a tendency to spend my spare time on pursuits that interest me, than spending time in prayer or Bible study or meditation.

And the pathway to recognising spiritual principles has not been all, plain sailing. Earlier in my life, I spent three years studying in a liberal theological college. There, the spiritual side of the faith was either ignored, or belittled. In the Theological College, it was implied that those who have a relationship with Jesus or God - those who were "born of the Spirit" - were weak-minded individuals who clutched at encounters with the Father/Son and Holy Spirit in order to help them cope with life's challenges and difficulties. Rather than face these problems alone, and work through the problems by self analysis.

Sad to say, I was very influenced by that type of insinuation, and for many years after my time in the theological college, had little time for or regard for; the spiritual side of our faith including: prayer, praise, worship and meditation.

What helped change that negative attitude towards the spiritual side of the Christian faith, was the way God graciously and sovereignly arranged a series of events to help me out of a health/financial crisis. I later calculated the possibility that this series of events (that solved our financial/health crisis) could have occurred by chance, was about,   5 million to 1.

After that series of events, I was left with a choice. Either I had could stubbornly hold to the idea that the series of events occurred by chance, or. Believe that the series of events occurred because a loving, living God had arranged these events, as if to say

> "Philip. You can leave me on the shelf, if you choose to. I won't force you but. You can have a relationship with me and a relationship with the risen Jesus and the Holy Spirit. We all love you"

Since then I have come to appreciate and

value, 'every' aspect of our human nature that is made in the image of God. Our physical body. Our intellect. Our emotions and the spirit that God gave us. And it wasn't just the 5 million to 1 series of events, that pulled my thinking away from depreciating the spiritual side of our nature and faith and towards, honouring and valuing the spiritual side.

In the years after the time in the theological College, we attended a caring Charismatic Church. There were no Bible thumping preachers in that church. Just leaders who intelligently taught the Bible and its' application to real life and the community around us. As I attended that church, from time to time I would notice that something the Pastor said, rang a bell in both my mind and spirit. Or there were times when I was reading a book written by a Christian (my mother kept giving me a seemingly endless stream of books to get my spiritual life, back on track), and something the author wrote, struck a chord. As that occurred, I gradually began to recognise that the *Spirit* (Holy), was speaking to *spirit* (mine).

It took about 15 years to fully peel away all negativity towards the spiritual side of the faith, and then to embark on a new pathway. A new pathway with a new mindset. A mindset that said. I take a very positive view of 'every' part* of the wonderful nature God has given us – including the spirit. Eccl 12:7 & Rom 8:16. And it is because we have been given a spirit, we can tune into, the Father/Son and Holy Spirit.

*God made us mind, body, spirit, emotions. God also made us sexual and social beings. Each part of our nature needs to be honoured.

One final thought in this introduction. The Apostle Paul wrote, "But it was to us that God revealed these things by his Spirit. For his Spirit searches out everything and shows us God's deep secrets. 1 Cor 2:10 NLT It is implied by those words "God's deep secrets" that a person can have a surface relationship with the Father and Son and Holy Spirit, or have a 'deep' relationship and it is implicit in this verse and other verses, that they want us to have a deep relationship with them, the only question being. Is that what we want to?

> *"Lord. Please open my spiritual eyes to see what you see, and my spiritual ears, to hear, what you hear. Amen."*

NB There are no chapters in this book. Instead, the spiritual insights and principles found in this book, have been grouped under the following headings:

The Father

1   DRAW NEAR TO GOD, AND HE WILL DRAW NEAR TO YOU

It is a principle. If we draw near to God - he 'will' draw near to us, whoever we are. God is, always faithful and always reliable and because of that characteristic of his nature, whenever a person turns their thoughts towards God; he will move towards that person; like the father of the prodigal Son - who came running towards him, when he saw him in the distance.

2   BE STILL AND KNOW THAT I AM GOD

This principle, is closely tied to the last principle. At some stage in our day, we need to slow down enough to be still or, still our thoughts for a few moments, to tune in to what the Father might wish to say. It could be anywhere, anytime. In the car or in a room or by a park. It could be while we are standing or sitting or even lying down. It could be after a period of praise and worship or reading the Bible or meditation. When we are still for a period of time, it just happens, we 'know' that he is near and he is our God.

3   HE LEADS ME BESIDES THE STILL WATERS AND RESTORES MY SOUL Psa 23:2-3

Sometimes we need to get away from it all, to hear God's voice more clearly – and to be restored. It could be by still waters, or it could equally be in the countryside or hills or mountains or the seaside. Being away and being still, is sometimes the best place, to hear his voice. Sometimes, for our soul to be restored, we need to step back or sideways from our busy life – for stepping back or sideways, is the best way to go forward.

When we make a point of being beside

the still waters/countryside or park; it allows us to peel off the layers of responsibility or problems or confusion – and let God restore us. Jesus often did that. He often went away alone to pray. When our soul is restored then our *spirit* starts to sing also; and our mind is released, and our strength is returned.

4   THAT STILL, SMALL VOICE

That is usually how God speaks, in a still small voice. Even though he could thunder at us from heaven, God usually speaks in a quiet voice, as if asking, are you listening? When Elijah was in the desert, having fled from the threat of Queen Jezebel, he was waiting for God to speak. First of all a terrific winds passed, but God was not in the wind. Then an earthquake occurred and God was not in the earthquake. Then a fire came, but God was not in the fire. Finally, God whispered to him. 1 Kings 19:13

5   MY THOUGHTS ARE NOT YOUR THOUGHTS DECLARES THE LORD AND MY WAYS ARE NOT YOUR WAYS , DECLARES THE LORD. Isa 55:8

I have learnt over the years, that God will work everything for good with those who love him but He will do it 'his' way, which may not necessarily be, our way. God doesn't try to tease human beings with a plan that is different from ours, just for the sake of being different. If it is different is because of a number of factors. He knows us better than we know ourselves. God's ways are often different to our ways; because:

1. He loves us and has our best interests at heart.
2. God knows everything.
3. God has unparalleled wisdom.

If we consider those three truths together, we might think it a smart move to ask God to guide us his way, the best way. The very next verse reads.

"For as the heavens are higher than the earth, so are my ways, higher than yours."

The best illustration of what that verse means, is to imagine that you are in a search party looking for someone who is lost in a wilderness area. The search party has scoured many square miles of countryside, looking for the lost person in thick undergrowth, and it seems an almost impossible task to find the lost person.

Overhead, is a search and rescue helicopter, and the crew have high-powered binoculars with infared sensors that can pick up warm blooded animals and humans. Suddenly, the pilot of the helicopter radios through and says. "We can see the person you are looking for. Just go forward 100 yds/m in a north-east direction, then go around the corner of a large rock, and look by a dark green bush. You will find the lost person, there."

It was the view of the crew from high up, that helped the search party on the ground locate the missing person. It is the same, with God our father. His ways may be different from ours and are better, simply because God can see the 'bigger picture', from on high - like the crew of the helicopter with special sensors and binoculars.

6   FOR WHOEVER COMES TO GOD MUST BELIEVE THAT HE EXISTS AND REWARDS THOSE WHO SEEK HIM Heb 11.6

There are obviously, two stages of belief. (1) That God exists (2) God rewards those who seek him. We don't go to God just to get, never-the-less, God loves it when we not only believe he exists but also believe that he has our best interests on His heart and consequently and will give us what we need – and many of our desires.

7   IF YOU 'EARNESTLY' SEEK HIM Psa 63:1

God does not want us to strain and shout and badger him, but sincerely and persistently seek his will and guidance and provision. When we do that, we will find his answer.

8   SEEK GOD'S FACE, NOT JUST HIS HAND 2 Chron 7:14

Sometimes, God wants us to love him for who He is and to seek his face, not just when we need something from His hand. I make this analogy. Do you have a friend who only comes around to your place, when they need something? Eventually, only the most gracious would continue to welcome that sort of friend. Someone who only contacts you, when they need something. God is the same. He loves to meet our needs, but is even more delighted when we come to him, just to enjoy being in his presence – or to praise and worship him.

9   SEEK 'FIRST' THE KINGDOM OF GOD, AND HIS RIGHTEOUSNESS, AND EVERYTHING ELSE WILL BE YOURS AS WELL. Matt 6:33

The principle here is about our priorities in life? Through those words, Jesus was challenging the disciples to consider their priorities in life. Not everything else first, and the Kingdom of God; second, third or ninth. Jesus words create this question. Does your my life and my life, revolve around:

Me, or we and Thee?

10   GOD WILL GIVE US OUR NEEDS Phil 4:19

God is too wise to just give us everything we 'want' in the same way that a caring parent will not give a young child, everything they want. A young child may enjoy some chocolate, then ask for more. After they have eaten the extra chocolate, may ask for, even more! At some stage, most caring parents will say to the child. "That is enough for now".

Saying "no" to that child, is actually a sign of the parent's love and maturity. Likewise, God will not give us everything we want, but will give us most of what we want, and everything we need.

11   GOD IS A GOD OF 'BOTH', THE HILLS AND VALLEYS

King Benhadad's officials said to him, "The gods of Israel are mountain gods, that is why the Israelites defeated us. But we will certainly defeat them if we fight them on the plains. .... A prophet went to King Ahab and said., "this is what the Lord says : 'because the Syrians say that I am a god of the hills and not the plains, I will give you victory over their huge army, and you and your people will know that I am the Lord. 2 Kings 20: 23 & 28 (G.N)

The spiritual principle that is found in the prophets words, is this. God, the creator, is not confined or restricted to, any place on Earth. He is a God of both, the hills and the valleys. He is the God at our Church and equally, our home or place of work. He is God when everything is peaceful and equally those times, when we have hassles and difficulties and unresolved issues. God is a God of 'both', the hills and the valleys! The night and the day. Home and work and recreation.

12   YOUR 'WILL' BE DONE ON EARTH AS IT IS IN HEAVEN

This is the principle that defined Jesus' life. He said, "my food is to do the will of Him who sent me." He sought out disciples who would had exactly the same desire. That is why he taught them to pray, the above words.

It is not always easy to determine the will of God, but it is more important that we have the desire to do the will of God, rather than have a perfect record in getting it right - all the time. It is our attitude, that is all important to God. That we live our life with the attitude, 'I want to do your will - and not my own'.

13   'WAIT' UPON THE LORD Psa 27:14

This principle ties in with the last point. We may want to do God's will, and even know what he wants us to do – but there may be a further restraint. He (because of his great wisdom) may ask 19.5us to 'wait' for his timing. Jesus said at the beginning of his ministry, "My time has not yet come." John 2:4. Near the end of his ministry he said, "Father the time has come." John 17:1 So waiting for God's timing is important.

Then there is, waiting upon the Lord. As we take time out to be quiet, we might not immediately sense his presence but we will as we spend time. More importantly, our spirit will be tuned for the day so we will be more receptive to his voice or prompting. We will know he is present, even as the waves splash on our foreshore.

14   WE CAN BE HONEST WITH GOD

We can be honest with God. In fact he prefers it that way. David was honest with God. He wrote, "How long, O Lord? Will you forget me forever? How long will you hide your face from me? Psa 13:1 NIV

There are a number of similar examples.

"Why, O Lord do you stand off? Why do you hide yourself in times of trouble? Psa 10:1 When a person has trouble or frustrations, it is better to be honest with God. If necessary, tell him you are angry. God has huge shoulders and a big heart and can handle our complaints or anger – if we feel abandoned by God, like David did.

15   GOD WANTS A RELATIONSHIP WITH US

The word relationship is not found in the Bible, but it is a summary of points 1-14. God does not want us to treat him as a being who is worshipped on Sunday and then forgotten Monday to Saturday. He created us for a relationship with him and wants us to have a relationship with him, 24/7. Some have explained it this way. We have a God-shaped vacuum in our lives and though people try and fill that vacuum with all sorts of substitutes, the only thing that will really fill that vacuum, is a relationship with our God – our maker. That is why Jesus called God "father" and David called him a "shepherd".

If the content of the Bible could be summarised in a few paragraphs, it would be like this.

Adam and Eve had a continuous and natural relationship with God, so there was no need for a special place like an altar, to meet with God. After the fall, that natural fellowship was broken and people had to 'seek' a relationship with God. A close relationship was still possible, but people had to seek that relationship – had to work at it.

The people we meet between the books of Genesis and Revelation had various degrees of relationships with God. Their relationship varied between non-existent and very close. Only Jesus had a total relationship with God.

The book of Revelation looks forward to the time when again, either in heaven or on the new Earth, human beings will have continuous fellowship with God and they will experience God like Adam and Eve did before the fall. I.e. God being everywhere present and there will be no need for a Temple or Church because the presence of God will be, everywhere present.

In a quality human relationship, both parties talk to each and other and listen to each other. That is what God wants. That is what Jesus wants and the Holy Spirit wants. For us to talk with them. Tell them what is on our heart and four us to listen to them and hear what is on, their heart, for there to be a two way conversation of relationship.

In the Bible, the relationship between God and human beings has been formalised in what is called a 'covenant relationship' – with blessings for both parties and responsibilities for both.

Jesus

16   JESUS KNOCKS ON OUR DOOR – BUT WE MUST OPEN IT Rev 3:20

It is amazing. The Son of God knocks on the door to our lives and graciously waits for us to open it. He could get anyone of his angels to, force the door to our lives open. An angel could easily break the locks on the door to our lives, so Jesus could come in, whether we like it or not. Instead of forcing a break-in, Jesus quietly knocks at the door of our lives; waiting, waiting, waiting - for us to open the door. We can and sadly many do, just leave Jesus standing there, as if to say. Thank Jesus, but I've got other priorities, why not try another door?

17   HE DESIRES TO HAVE FELLOWSHIP WITH, YOU AND I Rev 3:20

When we do open the door, Jesus comes in to have fellowship with us which is another word for relationship. When Jesus was on this Earth, he spent some of his time teaching but much of it was spent around tables in fellowship with people. In the Gospels we picture him a the home of Mary and Martha, eating and talking with them or at the house of a Pharisee. He invited himself to the house of Zacchaeus and talked with Zacchaeus and his family. We know he spent time around the table with his disciples.

The risen Jesus is the same. He wants friendship and fellowship with you and I. Some say, "all religions are the same". That statement is based on ignorance. In Bhuddism for example, there is no God. Christianity is the only religion in which the saviour comes seeking and knocking, and the only religion where grace is the predominant characteristic. Christianity is the only religion in which the God, seeks a relationship of friendship and fellowship with human beings, despite humans being mortal and vastly inferior in power and knowledge.

Christianity is, at it's best, a series of relationships and amongst the special relationships, is a relationship with Jesus. That is why he prayed for the disciples that they would have the same type of relationship he had with the Father. "I in them and you in me..." John 17:23

18   REMAIN IN ME AND I IN YOU John 15:7

This verse is closely linked to the previous verses. In the book of Revelation, Jesus knocks at the door or our heart, asking us to open the door. Opening the door, is our choice and once we have opened the door open, through the words above, it is as if Jesus was saying. I would love you to keep the door of your heart open, for the rest of your life.

19   IF YOU CONFESS JESUS AS LORD Rom 10:9

After Jesus came to dine at Zaachaeus house, Zaachaeus called him "Lord". It is appropriate to confess those words at the beginning of our Christian journey, but also along the way. To say, "Jesus is my Lord" or "you are my Lord" for it affirms to our mind and soul and spirit, who is Lord.

Speaking the words "I love you" to a partner, helps cement the relationship and likewise. Confessing the words "Jesus is Lord", helps cement our relationship with him but also declares to the spiritual powers who we belong to and who is in control of our lives.

20   LORD OF ALL

To be truly Lord, Jesus must be Lord, of 'every' area of our life. Of our recreational activities, business activities, our work, our dealings with our neighbours and friends and strangers. If Jesus is not Lord of all, he is not Lord, at all.

21   BATHE IN JESUS' INCREDIBLE LOVE FOR YOU

"I pray that...you..may have power....with all the saints....to grasp how wide and long and high and deep is the love of Christ, and to know that love... Eph 3:16-19 (abbrev) NIV The love of Jesus for each Christians is what is so special and different about the Christians faith. Bathe in that love.

Holy Spirit

22   WE HAVE NOT RECEIVED THE SPIRIT OF THIS WORLD BUT THE SPIRIT WHO IS FROM GOD, THAT WE MAY UNDERSTAND WHAT IS FREELY GIVEN US 1 COR 2:12

Just two points here. There is no equivalent to the Holy Spirit in any other religion. Secondly, the prime reason the Holy Spirit has come; is to be our - helper. Our helper in so many different ways. To convict us, if necessary. To comfort us, when needed. To guide us, when unsure of the way. To teach about Jesus. To remind us of Jesus words and

Scripture. To assure us. To give us joy. To give us faith. To inspire us. There are so many ways the Holy Spirit can help Christians, so pray today. "Please come Holy Spirit, my helper."

23   IT'S NOT BY MIGHT, NOR BY POWER, BUT MY SPIRIT SAYS THE LORD
Zech 4:6

Person 1, achieved their goal; this way. I had a vision. I did research into the market. I made plans. I and others did the preparation work; and the vision became a reality.
(That vision was achieved by someone whose life, centered around me)
Person 2 also achieved their goal, this way.

The Holy Spirit gave me a burden for what was on, God's heart. The Holy Spirit prompted me to act, and then guided me as the plans were drawn up. At each step along the way, I sought the wisdom of God, and the guidance of the Holy Spirit. C.f. Rom 8:14. As a consequence of seeking the Spirit's guidance and help, the vision became a reality. "It was not by might, nor by power, but by God's Spirit working through us, that the goal was achieved."

24   WHOEVER IS LED BY THE SPIRIT OF GOD, IS A SON OR DAUGHTER OF GOD Rom 8:14

This verse, is a partner verse to the verse above. Many tasks in the kingdom of God, are obvious. As a pastor said. "I was at an elderly woman's house; and she told me. Because of my poor health, I can't take the rubbish to the gate and the person who normally does it, has not turned up." He said. "I didn't need to pray about, what I should do next." That is like many tasks in life and the kingdom of God. We don't need guidance, a voice speaking from heaven, to do the obvious.

But sometimes, tasks in the kingdom of God, are not obvious, and that is where the leading of the Holy Spirit is important. An example is found in the book of Acts.

"The Spirit told Philip, "Go to that chariot and stay near it." Acts 8:29 In the story found in the second part of Acts chapter 8. Philip obeyed the voice of the Spirit; and followed up by asking an obvious question of the important official.

Over the centuries, many prayers have been prayed. Phone calls, made. Money given. Practical assistance offered. Hospitality offered or words spoken,   because Christians have responded to the prompting of the Holy Spirit. These prayers, calls, gifts, practical assistance and words have been prayed/made/spoken when there has been 'no obvious reason' to do them.

The reason the Holy Spirit has prompted Christians to do the tasks above, is that Holy Spirit has seen a need; and looked around for someone to meet that need. When we are sensitive to the Holy Spirit's prompting, we are as Paul wrote, son's and daughters of God.

25   BE FILLED WITH THE SPIRIT Eph 5:18

Those words are, present tense continuous, meaning. Paul wrote those words to encourage us to ask to be filled with the Spirit every day. When we ask, he comes. NB Most of the time Christians who ask the Holy Spirit to fill them, do not 'feel' his presence in any significant way, but during the course of the day, they will. That is why it is important to ask in faith. NB The Holy Spirit desires to fill us, much more than we desire the Holy Spirit to fill us.

Many who ask the Holy Spirit to fill them each day, do not feel any different, initially. If so, I make this analogy – one that those who drive cars will find easy to understand. When a person is driving a car and it is getting towards night-time, they come into a period which some call twi-light or half-light. During that period of half-light, even though the driver has turned the lights on, they will not see any evidence on the road. The only evidence will be a small light on the dash, indicating the lights are on. In fact they are on, it is just that there is no obvious sign.

It is the same with the filling of the Holy Spirit. When we ask, he comes and fills our life afresh. But like the driver who has their lights on during the half-light, it may not be immediately obvious. However, when that driver get's to night-time, it will be obvious that they had turned their lights on because they will see the beams of light, shining on the road.

It is the same when we ask to be filled afresh, with the Holy Spirit. When we ask, we may not be initially aware of it, but inevitably during the course of the day, we will be more sensitive to the Holy Spirit and he close by, because we asked.

26   BE SENSITIVE TO THE HOLY SPIRIT

Paul wrote, "Do not grieve the Spirit". We grieve the Spirit when we get involved in sexual immorality, idolatry (NB our idols may be great wealth or power), selfish ambition, drunkenness, being conceited, or jealous. These actions and attitudes are listed between Gal 5:19-26, and are the opposite of what the Holy Spirit wants for our lives. It grieves him, when we do these things.

What the Holy Spirit does want, is for us to sow to the Spirit.

27   SOWING TO THE SPIRIT. Gal 5:16

Sowing to the Spirit includes a number of actions: Listening to worshipful or faith inspiring, Christian music. Thinking about good things. Honouring people. Speaking encouraging words. Speaking words of understanding. Speaking words of truth. Speaking positive faith-building words. Giving to others. Being still before God. Reading the Bible. Praying. Listening to a good speaker. Reading an inspiring story or an inspired book. Obeying what the Lord has told us to do. Waiting for the Spirit's prompting.....

Warfare

28   (Defensive) THE ANGELS OF THE LORD ENCAMP AROUND THOSE WHO FEAR HIM. Psa 34:7

In a time of danger, remind yourself of this. No person or circumstance is a match for any angel who is with you. If threatened or feeling threatened, remind yourself by quoting God's word. "The angels of the Lord are around me."

29   (Offensive) THE SWORD OF THE SPIRIT IS THE WORD OF GOD Eph 6:17

Jesus used this weapon. Speak God's word into your situation. "My God will supply my needs." "I can do all things through Christ who strengthens me." "The battle is not mine, but God's." E.t.a.

30   THE WEAPONS OF OUR WAREFARE ARE 'MIGHTY' 2 Cor 10:4

These weapons include the blood of Jesus (defensive) and the word (offensive) which we exercise by our choice, using our faith. These are, mighty weapons! Effective weapons. Amen

31   TAKING EVERY THOUGHT, CAPTIVE TO OBEY CHRIST 2 Cor 10:5

We are the driver of our own car. We control, who comes into our house or flat. We choose what internet sites we go to. We choose the clothes we wear. We can also choose what stays in our minds.

Because we live in the world and because Satan is our adversary, sometimes thoughts will come into our minds that are from satan, or there are negative thoughts that others have spoken to us or a negative thought, from whatever source, has become resident in our mind.

Essentially Paul was urging the Christians at Corinth, to throw negative or condemning thoughts out, like the rubbish. To take hold of thoughts not from Jesus, and throw them out.

The principle weapons of satan's cronies are: doubt, discouragement and lies. They may employ a number of strategies (the Apostle Paul called them schemes Eph 6:11) to derail our relationship with Jesus and with God the father. One strategy is to adopt a libertarian stance and the other is to adopt, a legalist stance.

The aim of the first stance, is to derail Christians into doing things against the moral teachings of the Bible, while the legalist stance is to discourage Christians by attempting to make them feel condemned or second rate - usually over something very minor. Or for a Christian to feel condemned about some sin or action, that is already forgiven and forgotten. I.e. A confessed sin cannot be forgiven twice. Once is enough for God to forgive and forget any sin – for after confession, God presses the delete button.

If they adopt a libertarian role, they

might implant a thought such as. 'It doesn't matter if you watch pornographic images on the computer. A little pleasure, is not going to hurt. Or it doesn't matter if you take property from work without your employer's knowledge. That's the libertarian line, "it doesn't matter".

Or if they adopt a legalist position, they may implant a thought in our mind such as 'You slept in on Sunday and didn't get to Church. You really are, only a second-class Christian! Real Christians (the ones who God and Jesus love), are those who set their alarm and make sure they get to Church, tired or not.'

Then, if demons are having sway in our minds, they might continue in the same vein. The first-class Christians, are the ones God really loves. He answers their prayers, straight away. However, because you are 'only' a second or third class Christian, maybe God will eventually get around to listening to your prayers - who knows?'

Doubt and uncertainty and worry, are their usual methods. We need to reject such thoughts by quoting Scriptures such as. Romans 8:1 or Eph 2:8&9 or Jeremiah 31:34

Sin, the blood of Jesus, and confession

**32   ..FOR ALL HAVE SINNED, AND FALL SHORT OF THE GLORY OF GOD.
ROM 3:23**

If we want a close relationship with the Father/Son and Holy Spirit, we need to acknowledge that sin clouds our relationship with the Father/Son and Holy Spirit. But confession of our sin, blows the cloud away. The word 'sin' means, missing the mark. An arrow can hit an archery board, but may be, well wide of the centre mark. That is how it is, with sin.

We can justify what we think and do but if we measure our thoughts and actions against a holy and perfect God (Rom 3:23); we will realise that we have sinned, and in doing so, have missed the mark. However, that is not the end of the story. The stain need not remain.

33   WITHOUT THE SHEDDING OF BLOOD, THERE IS NO REMISSION OF SINS Heb 9:22

Even though our minds may argue, why was it necessary for Jesus to shed his blood, for our sins to be forgiven - Jesus had to shed his blood, for our sins to be forgiven. It is a divine law. Without the shedding of blood, there is no remission of sins – and we are reminded of the fact that Jesus shed his blood, when we take the communion cup.

34   WITHOUT THE 'CONFESSION OF SINS, THERE IS NO FORGIVENESS 1 John 1:9

Charismatic and Pentecostal Churches, no longer have a liturgical style of service - which in their eyes, often has become, a ritual. Those same churches, pride themselves that they teach from the Bible - God's word. What most of these churches have not recognised, is that when they discarded the liturgical type of service - they discarded two key teachings from the Bible.

In most Pentecostal and Charismatic churches, the congregations do not confess their sins each Sunday, something which is part of a liturgical service. That is surprising because, the Bible makes it clear that we all sin, and therefore need to confess that sin! So where in the New Testament is the teaching found that we all sin?

The Apostle John wrote. "If we claim we have not sinned, we make him a liar and his word has no place in our lives." 1 John 1:10. John used the inclusive word 'we' and wrote these words near the end of a long and godly life. By using the inclusive word 'we', John was obviously including himself – an old and godly man. If we claim we do not sin, his 'word' is not in us.

The Apostle Paul wrote. ...for all have sinned and fall short of the glory of God. Rom 3:23 Note the word, "all". Then Jesus, the Son of God, made the same point. He said "If anyone of you is without sin.... John 8:7 Jesus spoke those words to Pharisees who made a point of meticulously observing all of the law.

Both John and Paul used the word "all", while Jesus used the word "anyone" to describe those who sin. So because the Apostles John and Paul, and the Son of God 'all' make the same point that we all sin, why do Christians in Churches that claim they base their teachings on the Bible, not confess their sins – particularly because they claim/believe what they teach, is based on the Bible?

At the same time he was making the point that we all sin, John wrote 'If' we confess our sins... then God will forgive us. 1 John 1:9 Jesus also encouraged his disciples to confess their sins when he taught them to pray "Forgive us our sins....Matt 6:12

Worship/praise

35   All NATIONS WILL COME AND WORSHIP BEFORE YOU. Rev 15:4

We humans were, designed to worship! We humans are designed to do a number of number of things naturally including: to pray, to give, to love and to worship. People of all races and personality types find that if they put themselves in the right place away from life's distractions (and particularly with music), they were made to worship. And one day, because the ability to worship is universal, all people from all nations, will worship God.

36   YOU INHABIT THE PRAISES OF YOUR PEOPLE. Psa 22:3

It is a spiritual law. When we begin to praise God. When we begin to praise Jesus, the presence of the Holy Spirit, comes. That is the inevitable result of praising God and praising Jesus, for who they are.

37   WHERE AND HOW, ARE NOT IMPORTANT. John 4:24

Jesus told a Samaritan woman....you will worship the Father neither on this mountain nor in Jerusalem. John 4:21 NIV Jesus was meaning. Where, is not important. We can praise God in church, or in a car or at home or as we walk. Where, is not important. We can praise him with our hearts, our voices, with our hands and with our bodies.

38   WORSHIP HIM IN SPIRIT AND IN TRUTH John 4:24

The where, is not important, nor is the how! Standing or kneeling or sitting or lying down. Nor is the type of music. The type of music that each congregation or denomination prefers is not important.

From what Jesus said, what is important to God, is our heart-attitude. What is important to God is that when we worship and praise, we don't care what others think. What is important is what is on our heart. That the Father and Son are 'worthy' of worship. See chapters 4&5 or the book of Revelation.

39   A SACRIFICE OF PRAISE HEB 13:15

In heaven there are no difficulties. There are no problems or down times or desert times. Here on earth however, sooner or later, we will have times like these. When they occur, sometimes our praises dry up. But the writer of the book of Hebrews wrote about bringing a 'sacrifice' of praise. That is, praise made during those (down/desert) times when the last thing we feel like doing, is praising God.

It is a spiritual principle, that when we do make that sacrifice of praise in the hard times, God is touched and we will find his help and his blessing. I can recall in the past reading a book (sadly I can't recall the name of the book) which included the experience of someone who had a vision of God in heaven and in that vision, saw God weeping!

He wrote, God was weeping because he saw a small congregation of Christians worshipping him. Christians who had so many problems and who could have been excused, if they had focussed on their problems - instead of intentionally setting out to offer a sacrifice of praise. The prophet Habakkuk, wrote. "Though the fig tree does not bud and there are no grapes on the vine........yet will I rejoice in the Lord." Hab 3:17-18

The Christian life

The Christian life has been compared to both a long distance race and a pilgrimage. So what are the principles that will help us, complete the journey? Sometimes there will be a journey within the journey. For example, a woman at our Church shared how, after decades as a Christian, she was finally began to be honest with herself and others. So that endeavour to be honest with herself and others, became a journey within the overall journey of completing the Christian race or pilgrimage.

40   START THE JOURNEY!

Abraham obeyed God, and started the journey. He and his wife did not know where they were going or that they would stop half-way. They did not know that God would speak to them, further along the journey. Or that angels would appear to them, along the way. They had to take the first steps and trust that God was already in the future and knew what lay ahead, and that this journey was all planned! For their part, all Abraham and Sarah needed to do was, 'start' the journey.
It is a spiritual principle that we take the first steps, even if the end result, is not clear.

41   ..BE BAPTIZED...Acts 2:38

After starting the journey, the next step is baptism. Jesus, even though he was the Son of God, was baptised. In the Great Commission, Jesus commanded the twelve to baptise all future disciples. Matt 28:19 Peter, when he spoke the first sermon of the Church, urged those listening to "repent and be baptised". Baptism, is such an important step for new believers.

Baptism is a symbol of dying to the old life and beginning the journey of the new life. It is a public declaration before other believers and God, that a person is committed to the pilgrimage. Something changes for good in a person's spiritual walk when they take that step of obedience. I.e. Jesus commanded that the new disciples be baptised.

42   DO NOT DESPISE, SMALL BEGINNINGS Zech 4:10

Whether it is taking the first step or beginning to rebuild the walls of Jerusalem as the Jewish exiles did on their return from Babylon – don't despise the small beginnings or putting the first stone in place. Don't let Satan or others get on your case and try and discourage you because the beginnings will; inevitably be small, inconspicuous and under resourced. In fact, don't despise anything small or small anythings! They are all important in the kingdom of God. See Jesus teachings about a cup of cold water.

43   THERE ARE SEASONS IN THE CHRISTIAN LIFE C.f. Ecclessiaties 3:1-9

Along the Christian journey, recognise that there are 'seasons' in your life and that each season is, *all part of God's plan for your life.* Sometimes it is the season to be involved in some form of ministry. Yet there are likely to be other seasons, which are equally part of

God's plan for your life, when there is a season of rest. A season to recharge your batteries. What season it is, is a matter of wisdom and listening to what the Spirit is saying.

44   DONT WORRY ABOUT WHAT I HAVE ASKED YOU TO DO TOMORROW, JUST CONCENTRATE ON WHAT I HAVE ASKED YOU TO DO TODAY

That is the essence of Jesus words, when he said, "Live one day at a time". Matt 6:34 God is the expert life planner (see above), and Jesus is the expert of time-management. The best way to manage time, is to live one day at a time - to do what he has asked us to do today and leave for tomorrow any unfinished tasks. To leave unfinished tasks, in God's hands. That is a walk of faith.

The preceding words of Jesus were. ...."do not worry about tomorrow." When we worry about tomorrow, the devil is pleased because he knows we have ceased trusting God (by worrying about tomorrow); and at the same time - we are doing a very good job of, ruining today.

45   EVERYTHING IS PERMISSABLE – BUT NOT EVERYTHING IS BENEFICIAL 1 Cor 6:12

You and I can spend a lot of time and

energy on some ' good things, but we have to ask. Is what I am spending time and energy on, a godly thing? Ask questions like. "Is the amount of time and energy I am spending on...... advancing your spiritual life? Is it good for the kingdom of God?

I believe we all need to do things that revive and refresh us, and for each person, that will be different. Watching T.V. may be for some, a welcome release after a days work. Some might have a hobby, that revives and freshens, them. Everything is permissible, but not everything is beneficial. The questions being. How much time out, what and when?

Take my wife as an example. She enjoys reading a good book. Sometimes she starts a book and quickly finds she is enjoying it. Then, soon after the start she puts the book down and says. "This book is full of people having affairs (cheating on their partners), and lying; and revenge! I don't want to read a book, full of that kind of activity."

Some of our activities may need to be cut away completely or reduced or enjoyed selectively.

46   GIVE THANKS IN ALL CIRCUMSTANCES 1 Thess 5:16

Giving thanks, changes our perspective. Giving thanks, releases us and releases God to work further in our lives.

47   COUNT YOUR BLESSINGS

There are two states, in which to count your blessings. One is where we are thinking. 'Janet and Joe have so much more than I do. Perhaps God loves them, more than he loves me? Hopefully at that point we will hear a quiet voice asking. "Have you counted your blessings?"

Secondly, we who live in developed countries, need to remind ourselves about all the material blessings we have, as standard. I can recall a Christian leader telling our congregation about the time he was invited into one-room house of a Christian woman in Africa. Her only furniture, was a basic metal pot which she used for cooking. She and her family slept on the floor. The only clothes they had, were the ones they were standing in. Yet this Christian woman, continually spoke of, all her "blessings"! Blessings, yes blessings.

Then there is another space we can move to, if we live a life of, counting our blessings. Jesus wants us to move on beyond that point and live a life of - sharing our blessings, with others. When we live a life of counting our blessings and sharing our blessings, life is full. That is life and Jesus will be able say to us at the end of our life. "Well done, good and faithful servant."

48   WEAR YOUR OWN ARMOUR. DO NOT TRY TO PUT ON SOMEONE ELSE'S ARMOUR

Another tip to complete the journey successfully, is. Don't try to wear someone else's armour or to use another analogy. Don't try to walk in someone else's, shoes. David tried to wear King Saul's armour, but found it was too heavy and did not fit properly. If we try to be like someone else, we will find their armour too heavy or their shoes, uncomfortable. Be comfortable with who you are. What gifts and opportunities God has given you.

I.e. We each have different strengths and weaknesses. Each have different gifts. Each have different callings. Just concentrate on your strengths, your gifts and follow the motivations, that God has put on, your heart.

49   WEAR THE BREAST-PLATE OF RIGHTEOUSNESS Eph 5:14

In this day, it is even more important

than ever that we wear the breast plate of righteousness. That our words are true. That every thing we do, is done with, uncompromising honesty. Satan can easily get through our armour, if we allow dishonesty or deceit into our lives but he cannot get through the armour of those who know they are walking with a righteous, breast-plate.

50   DO YOU AND I, HAVE A TEACHABLE SPIRIT?

We never really arrive in the Christian faith. We still have more to learn at each turn and each stage of the journey so it pays to keep, a teachable spirit.

51   DEDICATE EVERYTHING TO THE LORD SEE PHIL 4:6 & PROV 3:6

God knows in advance what our day will bring but he wants us to dedicate our day to him. To dedicate our work, our loved ones, our home, our finances; everything we own and do, into his hands. God knows in advance about our day, but still wants us to dedicate it to him. That places the day and all the coming events, in his hands. It is the same with our possessions. In a sense, everything we own belongs to the Lord, but he wants us to dedicate all we have, to him. Something takes place in the spiritual realm when we dedicate our day, our thoughts and all we own, into his hands. Life becomes richer and we become, freer because our day is not just me. It is thee and me and others.

52   FORGET WHAT IS BEHIND Phil 3:13

Paul wrote, "forgetting what is behind, I press on." We may have had great success or great difficulties in the past. Either way, in the Lord's economy, forget the past (not the lessons of the past) – and press on. As far as the Lord is concerned any successes or failures are in a past – but he is calling us today and towards, tomorrow.

53   EVEN IF YOU GIVE A CUP OF COLD WATER, YOU WILL NOT LOSE YOUR REWARD   Mat 10:42

There is the world's economy and then there is, God's economy. In God's economy we are always in debt - the debt to love others. See Romans 13:8. However, while human debts are a burden, his debt (to love), is a blessing. With this debt, we get paid, both in this life, and in the life to come. Giving, no matter how big or small is a deposit of goodness into someone else's life, and ultimately for our heavenly bank account.
The only motive for giving is to see someone's thirst slated. Their hunger satisfied. Their self esteem grow. For others to have opportunities, they

would not other-wise, have. When we do so, even though it is not our motive, our heavenly bank account, grows.

Implicit in the words of Jesus, is the value of small acts of love. To most people, a small act like giving a cup of cold water, is is merely that - a small act. But in God's economy that act and every act of kindness, has great value! It is not a 'merely, a cup of cold water. It was not a 'merely' a phone call you made because you were concerned about someone else.

It is not a merely ..... Every act that has someone else's welfare in mind, is of inestimable value, in the kingdom of God.

54   GIVE AND IT WILL BE GIVEN YOU LUKE 6:38

For Christians, giving is meant to be like - bread and butter. We don't give to receive but we will receive, if we give. You see it is a spiritual principle as well as a life-principle. When we give, either to the Church/Christian organisation/another person, a number of things happen.

God looks down from heaven with favour and says. "That is my daughter or son; who is giving". And Jesus looks down from heaven and says, "that is my disciple, who is giving." And we don't have to give a lot; to be a giving person. Jesus said, even if you give a cup of cold water, you will not lose your reward. Matt 10:42

When we give, it frees up our spirit. The spirit of this world is get, get, get... while the spirit of Jesus – is to give. The benefits are wider than just feeling good that you have blessed someone. Take a recent example from our house. My wife said, "I rang .....because she was, on my heart." That person, did not belong to our Church and was not a person who we had regular contact with, during the past 10 years however, she was "on my wife's heart".

Once my wife rang, she found out this person was going through a temporary period of physical and emotional difficulties - and was unable to work. My wife resolved to make her two meals, and when she turned up with these meals, they were very much appreciated, as was the thought. A former friend would care enough to spend time and money preparing meals, storing them and then bringing them over.

My wife could have said to herself. She's not part of 'our' Church, let her Church, look after her. Or my wife could have said to herself. Because we shifted away and regular contact had been broken, she is a 'past-friend' and I no longer need to care for her. However, the Father/Son and Holy Spirit, think differently. They look down from heaven, see a need and then ask. 'Who can meet that need?'

Other factors with this example. Giving is a beneficial life principle and it is also a spiritual principle, confirming we are son's and daughters of God - and citizens of heaven. But think about it from the perspective of the woman, who the Father and Son love. Maybe her prayer was. 'Dear God, I am struggling mentally, physically, emotionally and spiritually (and financially?) at the moment – do you still care?'

Then a former friend rings up and brings some meals over which helps out practically and financially – and is the answer to her question, 'do you still care?' From time to time God provides miraculously. More often than not it is thorugh someone who cared to respond to the prompting of God's spirit.

Then there is the dynamic that was at work in my wife. Most desire to led by the Spirit   of God, but we don't always get it 100% right.   However, next time someone is on her heart, she will be more confident in responding to the Spirit.

St Francis of Assisi hit the nail on the head. In giving, we receive.

55   WHEN YOU GIVE, DO NOT LET THE RIGHT HAND KNOW WHAT THE LEFT IS DOING

Jesus and the Pharisees, did many of the same things. The Pharisees prayed regularly and Jesus prayed regularly. They believed in giving and Jesus believed in giving. The huge difference, was in their attitudes. The Pharisees seemed to want to do these things, so that others would notice what they did while Jesus urged his disciples to do the same things, but so that others would 'not' notice – and only God would see. Matt 6:1-2

56   LOVE OVERCOMES EVIL Rom 12:21

A person who became a Christian said, "prior to becoming a Christian, if anyone put something over me, I spent months planning my revenge and I planned to make sure their misery, would be at least twice if not three times, the trouble that person caused me. That is one way to deal, with evil."

Most of us find it difficult, not to respond to harmful words and actions, with revenge or resentment. If we can but listen to the words of Jesus and seek to do good to those who have done or spoken evil to us. God will change the situation, our hearts and most likely the heart of the person who has done us evil. Even if not, we will; win the day.

This is a successful formula for life, like the previous one. Giving is better than getting and overcoming evil with love, is a thousand times better than revenge. Revenge, often invigorates the cycle of revenge. While love in return for evil, usually stops the cycle and drains the pot of anger.

57   WORDS CAN BLESS AND CREATE.

Aaron was told to give this blessing to the people of Israel.

THE LORD BLESS YOU AND KEEP YOU, THE LORD CAUSE HIS FACE TO SHINE UPON YOU AND BE GRACIOUS TO YOU, THE LORD LIFT UP HIS COUNTENANCE UPON YOU AND GIVE YOU HIS PEACE Num 6:22-27

Aaron could have thought those words, but God wanted him to 'speak' those words. Words only have power, once they are spoken and in this example, they were words of blessing.

58   WORDS OF FORGIVENESS, RELEASE US

Jesus said, "if you do not forgive men their sins, your father will not forgive you your sins." Matt 6:14

By forgiving those who have wronged us, we break the hold of wrong over our lives, and are able to move forward. It is not about letting people off the hook or excusing what they have done; but when we forgive them, as much as anything, we release our spirit, soul and mind - from their actions and allow God to continue, his work in our lives and theirs.

59   WORDS MADE REAL, BY LOVE

The Apostle Paul wrote I"f I speak in the tongues of men and of angels but have not love, I am only a resounding gong." 1 Cor 13:1

Christianity is a religion of love. Paul wrote at the end of the same chapter which started with the words above. . "And now these three remain: faith hope and love. But the greatest of these is love." 1 Cor 13:13

It may be necessary to rebuke someone, but if it is, do it out of love. It may be necessary to say to someone, '"your sinful life-style is hurting yourself and others" – but do it out of love. Everything we do, we can do in love. In the spiritual realm, that is all, that will last.

60   NO ONE CAN SERVE TWO MASTERS..... YOU CANNOT SERVE BOTH GOD AND MONEY. Matt 6:24

Having money, is never a problem. Regardless of whether a person has a modest income or a high income, money 'can' be something people worship, love and trust in. Possessing money only becomes a problem when we start to desire it above: life and love and people and God. Soon after that, it becomes our god and then our master. And when that occurs, people begin to serve the real God with less and less passion and sadly once that process is complete, most fall away completely. When making money becomes such a priority in a person's life that it becomes a master. Gradually it draws people into it's, soul-destroying kingdom.

Resolve instead, to make all the money you can but at the same time. Love God and people more, and use money for your own needs and the kingdom of God.

61   GOD'S PLAN IS THAT WE BE SALT AND LIGHT

We ought to be, 'wowed' by these words, with this thought. I have the privilege of being salt and light in the world.

Faith

Faith is the currency of the kingdom of God. Expect God to listen. Expect God to move. Expect God to do a miracle. If our faith is seemingly small, pray for more faith. The first disciples said to Jesus, ''Lord increase our faith!'' Luke wrote that "Philip was filled with the Holy Spirit and faith." So pray, "Holy Spirit, please fill me more and more so that I will have, more faith."

Another way our faith grows, is through time with the Lord and time in the word. When we spend time alone with the Lord and his word, we may not feel an extra level of faith at that time but next time faith is required, faith will come easier. Our faith also grows as we exercise, our faith. When we get out of the boat so to speak – and start walking.

62   FIVE LOAVES AND TWO FISH, ARE ALL HE NEEDS TO DO A MIRACLE. Luke 9:13

Jesus never asks us for what we don't have, to do a miracle. He only asks us for what 'we' do have. I.e. What is in our hands or in our house, before doing a miracle.

63   WE ARE SAVED, BY GRACE, THROUGH FAITH Eph 2:8&9

It is at the centre of the Gospel, that we are saved by faith, in the shed blood of Jesus and by accepting Jesus as our Lord. We are not saved by attending Church, or praying, or cleaning up our act. They are natural responses to the salvation, so freely given.

Once we have been on the journey of faith for a while, most Christians need to come back to this well, and drink from it again. That is because, once we have been on the journey for a while, many have subconsciously slipped into a pattern of earning salvation. Perhaps even thinking we have fallen outside of salvation because we have slipped up in some way. Or that our salvation is being earned by regular Church attendance. Neither is true. We have been, are, and will continue to be saved by grace and through faith, in the shed blood of Jesus.

We are 'continually saved, by faith. It is only people who intentionally turn away from the Lord, who put themselves out side of salvation, but not grace. Grace will be extended, till the end of their lives.

64 OPEN YOUR MOUTH AND I WILL FILL IT. Psa 81:10

Some people are waiting for God to force open their mouth, so that they can be sure it is God speaking through them. God has another way of doing things. He wants us to take a step of faith and start speaking, and trust him to give us the words, once we have started speaking.

65 JESUS HAS BEEN GIVEN ALL AUTHORITY IN HEAVEN AND ON EARTH. MATT 28:18

After telling the disciples he had been given all authority on heaven and on earth; Jesus said to them. "Go and make disciples of all nations... 28:19. That means, we have been given the same authority. See also Mark 16:17-18

66   GO ANKLE DEEP, THEN KNEE DEEP, THEN GO, FAITH-SWIMMING C.f. Ezekiel Chapter 47

There is no limit to how deep a person, can go with God. There is no limit to the measure of the Holy Spirit, in our lives. It is, entirely up to us. Do we want to go, ankle deep? Or knee deep or thigh deep? Or, up to our waist or chest? If we were in water; and up to our neck and couldn't swim; we would possibly drown. If we go up to our neck in the spirit; we will be, totally alive. Enveloped in the love and the presence, and power of God.

67   DEEP CALLS TO DEEP Psa 42:7

This verse is related to the above verse. These words are not easy to explain. Through those words, David is saying – that the breadth and depth of the power and wisdom and knowledge of God, we earth-bound humans, will never fully, understand. We are un-equals in every way. Despite that, God graciously calls and invites us to share as much of his wisdom and knowledge, as we are capable of understanding. Deep calls to deep!

Prayer

**68   ASK AND IT WILL BE GIVEN YOU;
SEEK AND YOU WILL FIND; KNOCK
AND THE DOOR WILL BE OPENED.
Matt 7:7**

Joyce Meyer said,
*"It is a principle of God that even
though He knows what we need, He
still wants us to ask him for it."*

With apologies to Joyce Meyer. I can't
identify the particular radio message
that I heard her say these words, but
she said it, exactly right. The second
point that is implicit in Jesus words, is.
Ask specifically for what we want.

69   ..IF YOU BELIEVE YOU HAVE RECEIVED IT, IT WILL BE YOURS. MARK 11:24

To believe is to receive.

70   BE PERSISITENT LUKE 11:5-11

Being persistent in prayer; is the message of the parable Jesus told that is found in Luke's Gospel.

71   PRAY CONTINUALLY 1 THESS 5:17

Part of the privilege of being a Christian is that we can pray. More than that, we can   pray anywhere, any time – and continually.   We have God's spirit in us and so we are like, a walking Temple. We are able to pray where ever we go. I.e. Continually. In some religions, there is a set time for prayer; while for Christians the set time is every moment we are awake.

72   PRAY ABOUT EVERYTHING! Phil 4:6 LB

In the Living Bible, Paul's words are rendered. "Don't worry about anything; instead pray about everything... God knows about 'everything', so that is why the Apostle urged us to, pray about everything. God the father/Son and Holy Spirit are interested in, 'every' area of our lives. Finance, business, work,   recreation,   hobbies, relationships, difficulties e.t.a. When we pray about everything, we need to remember. (1) God knows about everything. (2) God cares (3). God 'will' make a change; for good.

73   FIND A ROOM

Jesus said, "But when you pray, go into your room, close the door and pray. Sometimes, we need to find a place where we can close out, all the other distractions of life, by closing the door of a room to the radio: T.V., phone or whatever distractions there are in our lives. See Matt 6:6

74   IF TWO OF YOU SHALL AGREE Mat 18:19

Unity is a precious commodity in heaven and the kingdom of God. It exists in heaven.   God values unity. When two or more agree in prayer about a request, the request is three or four times more powerful than if an individual prayed.

75   EARNEST PRAYER Jam 5:16

Wrote James, "The earnest prayer of a righteous person has great power. James 5:16 God takes more notice of, earnest prayers than a casual prayer like. Earnest does not mean straining. It just means, put your heart into it.

76   OF A RIGHTEOUS PERSON Jam 5:16

None of us are perfect, but if we endeavour to live a righteous life (a life on honest integrity) – the pathway of our prayers, is unhindered.

77   PRAYER AND FASTING Mark 2:20

The main person impacted by fasting, is us. God cannot be manipulated, and fasting will not achieve that. Nor is the devil defeated, because we fast. What changes, is our soul and spirit. We loosen the bonds of the food we so delight in, and because the bonds are loosed; that releases us to sense more clearly what God is saying to us. After fasting, Satan becomes satan, with a small 's'.

Guidance

78   PEACE Col 3:15

Only the Father and Son, can give us, true peace. Satan by contrast, is a restless being, so he cannot speak with peace or guide any person with peace. If we have a sense of peace, day after day about a future decision, that peace almost certainly comes from our loving shepherd. The Apostle Paul wrote. "The peace* that Christ gives you is to guide you in the decisions you make." Col 3:15 (Good News version)

79   YOUR WORD IS A LAMP TO MY FEET AND A LIGHT TO MY PATH. Psa 119:105

The Bible is one of the prime reference points, with guidance. It might be that a verse is illuminated, by the Holy Spirit. The Bible is also a lamp, because if we are not sure whether it is the Father/Son/Holy Spirit speaking to us. Run the thought, past Scripture. We will never hear the voice of the trinity, asking us to hold resentment against others, or kill someone, or be dishonest – because those actions go against the teachings of the Bible. On the other side of the coin, if we have an impression or hear a still quiet voice; asking us to bless someone. To pray for someone or give to someone; it is almost certainly from the Father, Son and Holy Spirit because those actions are consistent with the Bible.

Guidance is a big subject and can involve. Scripture, a peace that will not go away, advice from other people and circumstances.

80   THE FATHER/SON/HOLY SPIRIT, 'WANT' TO LEAD YOU'. Psa 23:2

Because God is like a caring shepherd, he wants to lead us and lead us by still waters. Then there is another factor We are capable of hearing his voice and knowing his direction. See also John 10:27

81   LEARN, TO BE LED

Amongst the least referred to words in the Bible outside the book of Leviticus, and amongst the most important, are these words. "I have learned." Phil 4:12 Paul was referring to the fact that he had "learned" to be content in whatever circumstances. He did not come into this life, 'programmed' to be content. He had to learn, to be content.

Likewise, we can learn to be led. The closer to the Lord we are and the more tuning we do, the easier it is but, at the end of the day, we have to 'learn' to be led and perhaps by making a few mistakes, along the way till we distinguish between our own thoughts and desires and possibly; satan trying to mislead us.

Keeping a diary may be helpful to review those times we got guidance right and identify the factors that contributed to that correct decision and of course those times we made a mistake.

Concluding thoughts

This book has not been an attempt to elevate the spiritual above other parts of our nature or imply that we float through this life like some, spirit-being, barely touching real life and real people and real situations. Jesus was our example. He was fully human (he got tired and frustrated and angry - he loved and laughed and enjoyed meals and happy occasions) and yet he was fully divine at the same time - and in constant touch with his Father and the Holy Spirit. For Jesus it was not an either or, but a both and...

The message of the Bible is that we

have been made in the image of God, who 'wants' a relationship with each person. Further, we have been given a spirit by God, making it 'natural' for us to relate to the Father/Son and Holy Spirit.

In the secular world, a relationship with the Father/Son/Holy Spirit is sometimes derided. At the root of that derision is a pride about their independence and in their self reliance. From my perspective, many pay a price for their pride and declaration of independence from God, turning to substitutes such as alcohol, cigarettes and drugs. Making causes or success, their gods. Trusting in money or other factors, as security. Turning to yoga and eastern religions. Becoming enamoured with secular philosophies, most of which are ultimately, empty vessels.

The message of this book is that we were made for (designed) a relationship with the Father/Son and Holy Spirit because we were made in the image of God. When we enter that relationship, life is complete and people find freedom. Further, those who understand the message of the Bible is that the Father/Son and Holy Spirit would like us to invite them into every sphere of our life. Personal. Relational.

Sporting. Cultural. Social. Business —
every sphere of life.

The relationship we can have with the
trinity now, is a foretaste of the God-
filled life we will experience in heaven;
after this short interlude on Earth.